WITHDRAWN

The One-Cent Tent

Pam Scheunemann

Consulting Editor, Diane Craig, M.A./Reading Specialist

ABDO
Publishing Company

Published by ABDO Publishing Company, 4940 Viking Drive, Edina, Minnesota 55435.

Printed in the United States.

Credits
Edited by: Pam Price
Curriculum Coordinator: Nancy Tuminelly
Cover and Interior Design and Production: Mighty Media
Photo Credits: AbleStock, Brand X Pictures, Photodisc

Library of Congress Cataloging-in-Publication Data

Scheunemann, Pam, 1955-
    The one-cent tent / Pam Scheunemann.
        p. cm. -- (First rhymes)
    ISBN 1-59679-499-2 (hardcover)
    ISBN 1-59679-500-X (paperback)
        1. English language--Rhyme--Juvenile literature. I. Title. II. Series.

PE1517.S435 2005
808.1--dc22
                                                                    2005047164

SandCastle™ books are created by a professional team of educators, reading specialists, and content developers around five essential components that include phonemic awareness, phonics, vocabulary, text comprehension, and fluency. All books are written, reviewed, and leveled for guided reading and early intervention reading, and designed for use in shared, guided, and independent reading and writing activities to support a balanced approach to literacy instruction.

Let Us Know

After reading the book, SandCastle would like you to tell us your stories about reading. What is your favorite page? Was there something hard that you needed help with? Share the ups and downs of learning to read. We want to hear from you! To get posted on the ABDO Publishing Company Web site, send us e-mail at:

sandcastle@abdopub.com

SandCastle Level: Beginning

-ent

cement

cent

dent

tent

vent

Look at the .

Here is a .

See the .

This is a .

This is a .

The truck is
full of cement.

A penny is one cent.

The car has a dent.

The tent is blue
and yellow.

**Air comes out
of a vent.**

The One-Cent Tent

Over in the
town of Kent
is a yard
full of cement.

In the cement in Kent
is a little vent.

From the vent
in the cement
comes a very
sweet scent.

A kind old gent
sees the vent
with the sweet scent
and puts up a tent.

tent for
rent 1¢

For only one cent,
the kind old gent
will rent the tent
by the little vent
with the sweet scent
that is in the cement!

About SandCastle™

A professional team of educators, reading specialists, and content developers created the SandCastle™ series to support young readers as they develop reading skills and strategies and increase their general knowledge. The SandCastle™ series has four levels that correspond to early literacy development in young children. The levels are provided to help teachers and parents select the appropriate books for young readers.

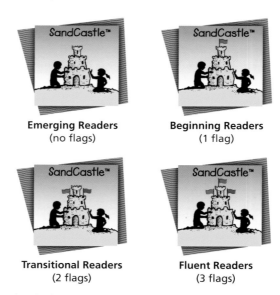

Emerging Readers
(no flags)

Beginning Readers
(1 flag)

Transitional Readers
(2 flags)

Fluent Readers
(3 flags)

These levels are meant only as a guide. All levels are subject to change.

ABDO
Publishing Company

To see a complete list of SandCastle™ books and other nonfiction titles from ABDO Publishing Company, visit www.abdopub.com or contact us at:
4940 Viking Drive, Edina, Minnesota 55435 • 1-800-800-1312 • fax: 1-952-831-1632